HO
HO
HO

ME!

HO
HO
HO

KISS ME!

ME!

KISS ME!

HO
HO
HO

KISS ME!

A Keepsake Book from the

HEART of the HOME

CHRISTMAS

JOY

MY BOOK

LITTLE, BROWN AND COMPANY

Boston · New York · Toronto · London

FIRST EDITION
ISBN 0-316-10682-8

FOURTH PRINTING

Published simultaneously in Canada
by Little, Brown & Company
(Canada) Limited

MANUFACTURED IN CHINA

TABLE of CONTENTS

and more . . .

"FOR SOMEHOW, NOT ONLY AT CHRISTMAS, BUT ALL THE LONG YEAR THROUGH, THE JOY THAT YOU GIVE TO OTHERS IS THE JOY THAT COMES BACK TO YOU."

♥ JOHN GREENLEAF WHITTIER

I've spent many years thinking about Christmas, my favorite holiday & a magical time of year on Martha's Vineyard, where I live. The colors, the twinkling lights, the cooking smells, the secrets, the fun; the sounds of Christmas: crackling fires, greetings of "welcome home", jingle bells, Santas & HO! HO! HO! all get my heart going pitter-patter. When I was little, the Christmas secrets were so overwhelming & I was so excited I would sometimes spontaneously burst into tears. So many days till Christmas morning!

When I was growing up, Christmas time for our large family (I'm the oldest of 8) added a kind of hysteria to the normal general commotion & when my grandma arrived on Christmas Eve in her big Chevrolet, the trunk LOADED full of presents, we almost went insane. Joy overflowed & got all over everything! All these years later we still laugh till we cry when we tell the stories.

I've "done" Christmas every which way I could think of — looking for the perfect balance between getting ready for it & enjoying it! For me it's a matter of priorities which is, very first, TIME, for family, for friends, for spirit & for community — none of the rest of it hardly matters at all. A heartful of peace matters, love matters, JOY matters. (COOKIES MATTER!)

This book is a collection of small ideas & tiny steps in the quest for a joyous & fulfilling Christmas & comes to you, with Love, from the Heart of the Home & me ...

♥ Susan Branch

RECIPE
FOR A
Happy Christmas

FILL A HOUSE WITH EQUAL PARTS OF
LOVE, HOPE, & PEACE

ADD THE JOY OF CHILDREN &
THE STRENGTH OF OLDER PEOPLE

SEASON WITH THE MUSIC OF
LAUGHTER & SOME
MISTLETOE KISSES

WARM BEFORE A CRACKLING FIRE
& SERVE WITH
OF COMFORT TIDINGS
& JOY!

O Winter, King of Intimate Delights...

HOME for CHRISTMAS

WITH POMP, POWER & GLORY THE WORLD BECKONS VAINLY,
IN CHASE OF SUCH VANITIES WHY SHOULD I ROAM?

WHILE PEACE & CONTENT BLESS MY LITTLE THATCHED COTTAGE,
AND WARM MY OWN HEARTH WITH THE TREASURES OF HOME. ♥

♥ BEATRIX POTTER

DECKING THE HALLS

Christmas is a magical time — think "magic" as you decorate your home. Shine up all your glass & silver to reflect the light — use shiny glass & sparkling things on the tree. Clean windows, mirrors, glass on pictures. Use crystal bowls to hold fruit & candy; glass candle holders, & elegant champagne glasses that ring like clear bells.

Use lots of candles — fat, thin, short & tall — everywhere. Set white votives in a bowl of coarse salt for "candles in the snow." Hollow out apples & put in candles. For parties & Christmas Eve, light the house mostly with candles, Christmas tree lights, & a fire in the fireplace — magic !

Sugared fruit: a very elegant & old-fashioned decoration or centerpiece — the fruit looks frosted & icy. Dip plums, red grapes, peaches, apples, etc. into egg white & roll in sugar. Put in a pretty bowl.

Drape garlands of pine over mantles, around mirrors, up stairs. Use boughs of holly, rosemary sprigs, English Ivy, poinsettias, mistletoe, paperwhites, pine wreaths, & clumps of baby's breath to decorate. Christmas trees in the kitchen, guest room, children's room.

Bowls of pinecones, apples, pomegranates, cranberries, holly, cinnamon bundles, whole nuts in their shells, tangerines & oranges studded with cloves. Simmer cloves, citrus peel, ginger, cinnamon & nutmeg for good smells.

Flowers: red & pink roses, white lilac, baby's breath, white tulips — something low, simple & elegant for the Christmas table.

Tape your Christmas cards around a doorway, window, or mirror.

8

Decking the Halls

Luminarias are usually made by putting sand in the bottom of a brown paper bag, then setting a votive candle in the sand. When lit, they make wonderful path lighters or front porch decorations. This year, at the last minute, I wanted one to greet guests on the porch, but I had no sand & no brown paper bag. I found a beautiful bag with the face of an angel on it & set the candle in grass seed! The light shone through & the angel face was beautiful. Later it came inside to decorate the hearth. ♥

A pumpkin cut with stars all over & lit with a candle is another fun porch light. Tie a wreath to the bumper of your car.

Play Christmas music ~ classical & "the boys" Frank, Bing, Dean & Nat.

Hang pictures of friends & family from previous Christmases on your refrigerator with little magnets. Set out the photo album to encourage remembrance. Set up framed pictures of family, especially those unable to be present. ♥

Candy houses, cinnamon hearts, chocolate kisses, plates of cookies, candy canes, ribbon candy, gingerbread houses, loaves of bread, popcorn balls & candied apples all perk things up. Use children's toys to decorate: blocks, trains & teddy bears.

For the table: a colorful quilt, a special lace tablecloth, or even a nice white bedspread. Hang stockings (with care) at fireplace or on backs of chairs.

Tie ribbon around the dog's neck, put a bell on the cat, dress up your children, put on a cute apron, send your mom a corsage, get dad a boutonniere, put jingle bells on the baby's shoes. Fill your house with love. ♥

9

THE FIREPLACE

In wintry places, the hearth is the natural gathering place for holiday celebrations — whether it be a festive tree trimming party, or just a cozy bowl of soup — in front of the fire is best. Keep your fire burning through the holiday season — it says welcome, come in, get warm! Here are some ideas:

The Yule Log:

I love this because it's whimsical, traditional & solemn all at once. Two weeks before Christmas everyone goes out to the woodpile to choose the biggest, most beautiful log to burn on Christmas Eve. Carry it into the house where it can be tied with a red ribbon & decorated with sprigs of rosemary (the symbol of friendship & remembrance). If you don't have a fireplace, it can be drilled with a hole, filled with a candle, & decorated with soap snow (p. 37). Display it on the hearth until Christmas Eve. Then, with great ceremony, burn the Yule Log (or light the candle) & all say a prayer to go up in the smoke. ♥

Fragrant Herb Bundles:

After using the leaves of your summer herbs, collect all the woody stems from basil, rosemary, thyme, & marjoram. Cut them to a uniform length & tie into bundles with ribbon or string. When packed into a basket with tiny pine-cones, the bundles make a sweet hearthside Christmas gift with a wonderful fragrance when burned. Save some for yourself! ♥

Cinnamon Spice:

Beribboned bundles of cinnamon sticks set near a warm fire will send off a delicious scent to fill the room with Christmas fragrance. ♥

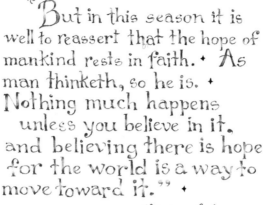

"But in this season it is well to reassert that the hope of mankind rests in faith. ⋆ As man thinketh, so he is. ⋆ Nothing much happens unless you believe in it, and believing there is hope for the world is a way to move toward it." ⋆

Gladys Taber

"Backward, turn backward
O Time in your flight;
Make me a child again
Just for tonight."

♥ Elizabeth Akers Allen

ON THE FIRST DAY OF CHRISTMAS VACATION, LET YOUR CHILD CHOOSE THE DINNER MENU. MAKE THIS A XMAS TRADITION. ♥

MAKE A "YAY! CHRISTMAS VACATION!" BANNER TO HANG OVER THE FRONT DOOR TO WELCOME THEM HOME. ♥

START A HOPE CHEST FOR BOYS AND GIRLS. PUT IN GREAT G'MA'S HAND EMBROIDERED DISH TOWELS, AUNT MARY'S FAMOUS SUGAR COOKIE RECIPE; ADD A STERLING SILVER PLACE SETTING EACH YEAR AND A SPECIAL BOTTLE OF WINE TO DRINK ON THEIR WEDDING DAY. PUT IN THEIR BABY BOOKS, KEEP-SAKES, PHOTOS AND MEMENTOS. HAVE FUN! ♥

ON CHRISTMAS EVE I USED TO RUN AROUND OUTSIDE WITH JINGLE BELLS AT THE WINDOWS — THE LITTLE KIDS WENT WILD WITH EXCITEMENT!

FILL YOUR CHILD'S CLOSET WITH BALLOONS ~ WRITE MESSAGES ON THEM ~ WATCH HIS EYES LIGHT UP.

HAVE A SPECIAL CHRISTMAS PARTY JUST FOR CHILDREN. A VINYL TABLE-CLOTH IS NICE — USE TINY TEDDY BEARS (FOR THEM TO KEEP) TO HOLD PLACECARDS. MAKE DECORATIONS, TAKE FLOWERS TO A CONVALESCENT HOME & SING SOME CAROLS, EAT CAKE & COOKIES, MAKE A CANDY HOUSE (THERE ARE KITS NOW), READ A CHRISTMAS STORY & PLAY PIN THE STAR TO THE TREE. SCAVENGER HUNTS ARE GREAT FOR OLDER CHILDREN. ♥

LOVE NOTE: MOM AND DAD MAKE A "JOEY SANDWICH" — THEY HUG EACH OTHER & PUT JOEY IN THE MIDDLE. ♥

LISTEN TO YOUR CHILDREN: SOMETIMES THEY'LL BE WANTING TO SHOW THEIR LOVE WHEN YOU ARE BUSY ~ TRY TO STOP AND RETURN THEIR LOVE WITH SPECIAL HUGS AND KISSES. ♥

WHEN YOU TAKE THEM CHRISTMAS SHOPPING, INCLUDE SOMETHING FUN JUST FOR THEM. TAKE TIME TO VISIT SANTA, SIT DOWN FOR A CHOCOLATE ECLAIR, LOOK AT DISPLAYS, OR SHOP FOR DADDY. ♥

BUNDLE UP YOUR CHILDREN AND TAKE THEM TO MIDNIGHT SERVICES (EVEN IF YOU HAVE TO WAKE THEM). IT CAN BE MAGICAL AND AWE INSPIRING. ♥

GIVE SOMETHING TO CHARITY EVERY YEAR AND DISCUSS IT ALL WITH YOUR CHILDREN. ENCOURAGE THEM TO BECOME CITIZENS OF THE WORLD. ♥

LET YOUR CHILDREN SNUGGLE INTO BED WITH YOU ON A SNOWY CHRISTMAS MORNING. ♥

MAKE A PHOTO ALBUM ESPECIALLY FOR YOUR CHILD FOR A CHRISTMAS PRESENT. STAR HIM, HIS FRIENDS, HIS PETS, HIM ON VACATION — IN-CLUDE CARTOONS, QUOTES, NEWS-PAPER HEADLINES, AND A BIG " I LOVE YOU." ♥

A SURPRISE BOUQUET OF FLOWERS WILL LET YOUR CHILD KNOW HOW SPECIAL SHE IS ♥. (OR HE IS.)

READ THEM A CHRISTMAS STORY, ONE CHAPTER EACH NIGHT — TO END THE DAY IN A RELAXING FAMILY ATMOSPHERE. ♥

CHILDREN ARE THE HOPE FOR THE FUTURE, SHOWER THEM WITH LOVE. ♥

"Children need Christmas trees, and not artificial ones either. The artificial ones have no fragrance, and some of them play tunes, which is dreadful to think of."

♥ Gladys Taber

A Loss of Innocence

I was _old_ when I found out about Santa Claus— I was twelve. At first I thought my mom kept it from me because she was afraid I'd tell the younger kids, but looking back, I think she just couldn't bear to break the news to me. I was _such_ a staunch supporter of not only Santa, but the elves & reindeers, Rudolph & Mrs. Claus & the brownies, & _everybody_. I fixed special food for them every Christmas Eve & they ATE it. Proof positive . ♥

Then one November day there was a gang of neighborhood kids in our house arguing quite vocally about the non-existence of Santa Claus. I was shocked at how _unbelievably_ dumb they could be, brazen morons really. I made it clear how I felt about their disloyalty & downright blasphemous attitudes: burnt cookies was all they'd be getting this Christmas. Of this, I was sure.

That evening my mother suggested we go for a ride in the car ALONE — unheard of in a family with 8 children. I knew something was up. But what?—what could it possibly be?

Staring out the window at the night stars, I listened quietly as she told me. After she finished there was a long silence, then my quivering voice asking "the Easter Bunny?" and she shook her head. Then the big one, the one I knew couldn't possibly be included in this hideous deception, "the Tooth Fairy?"

15

A Loss of Innocence...

All gone, swept away — all I had left were the princes & princesses (many of whom lived in trees in dark forests) in my fairy tale books, & I wasn't about to bring them up. I'd heard enough for one day.

Time has passed & I _am_ a grownup now. The truth _is_ that there ARE fairies & brownies; I don't care what anyone says. They live in the woods around my house, they keep fireflies as pets, & they help me write these books. Proof positive. ♥

CHRISTMAS CARDS & LETTERS

Mr. & Mrs. S. Claus
North Pole

Little Tommy Littlemouse
One Main Street
Wishtown, U.S.A.

STOP ALL DELIVERY

If you would like your Christmas cards to carry a more "authentic" postmark: address & put stamps on them; put them all in a large manila envelope & send it in care of the postmaster of one of these towns: North Pole, Alaska 99705; Santa Claus, Indiana 47579; or Christmas, Florida 32709. They will postmark your cards with the name of their town & send them out. Mail early!

Most post offices have "Santa's Elves" who personally answer children's letters to Santa — check with yours. Or, if you send them to North Pole, Alaska, they will be answered by the 6th & 7th grade writing classes at the North Pole Middle School. In Santa Claus, Indiana, there's an "elf" volunteer group to handle Santa's mail. On Martha's Vineyard we have Mr. Eddie Colligan, who takes the time to answer letters & grant the wishes of little ones. ♥

STOCKING STUFFERS

ALL KINDS OF LITTLE TOYS: JACKS AND BALL, A YO-YO, TINY TEDDY BEARS, A MAGNIFYING GLASS, CRAYONS, A SNOWSTORM IN A GLASS, A JUMPROPE, GLIDER PLANES, PADDLE BALLS, LITTLE DOLLS, WATERCOLORS AND BRUSHES, PAPER DOLLS, NOISE MAKERS, & STAR STICKERS. ♥

GIFT CERTIFICATES FOR FOOD, FLOWERS, AND FUN~ TICKETS FOR A PLAY, A CONCERT OR THE LOTTERY.♥

BEAUTIFUL OLIVE OIL, RED ITALIAN TABLE WINE IN A WICKER CONTAINER, ELEPHANT GARLIC, FANCY TEAS, MUSTARD, JAMS & POPCORN. A WHISK, MUG, VEGETABLE PEELER, KITCHEN SCISSORS, TWINE, OR MEASURING SPOONS.♥ RECIPES! ♥

BASEBALL, TENNIS BALLS, GOLF BALLS, HEAD AND WRISTBANDS, STOP WATCH, TAPE MEASURE, CALORIE COUNTER, BALLCAP, TICKETS FOR A GAME.♥

THINK OF HOBBIES AND GIVE ACCORDINGLY; GARDENING, SEWING, PUTTERING IN THE BASE- MENT, TRAVELING, READ- ING AND SO ON. ♥

BATHROOM STUFF: BUBBLE BATH, SWEET SOAPS AND LOTIONS, PERFUME, NAIL POLISH, HAIR CUTTING SCISSORS, SEASHELLS, DUCK- SHAPED NAIL BRUSH, A SHOWER CAP, AFTER SHAVE LOTION AND A HAND MIRROR. OH! AND HAIR RIBBONS, BOWS AND CLIPS ~ COMBS AND BRUSHES. ♥ (AND LOOFAHS AND SPONGES.) ♥

MITTENS, SOCKS, SCARVES, "DESIGNER" SHOELACES, SLIPPERS, AND A PAIR OF RED SILK BOXER SHORTS! BRACELET AND PINS AND EARRINGS~ AND A SILVER MONEY CLIP. LEATHER GLOVES, SILK STOCKINGS, AND A NEEDLEPOINT EYE- GLASS HOLDER. ♥

STATIONERY, BOOK PLATES, POSTAGE STAMPS, DIARY, PEN, PERSONAL CALENDAR, & TELEPHONE BOOK ~ GET THINGS MONOGRAMMED! ♥

GOOD SHARP SCISSORS, MAGNETS FOR THE REFRIGER- ATOR, TINY AMERICAN FLAGS, CHRISTMAS ORNAMENT WITH THE DATE ON IT, A TINY VASE, BED- SIDE CLOCK OR A MUSIC BOX.♥ CRYSTALS ARE BEAUTIFUL & PURPORTED TO TO BE MAGICAL.♥

"It is good to be children sometimes,
& never better than at Christmas."
♥ Charles Dickens ♥

THE BEST GIFTS ARE TIED WITH HEARTSTRINGS

The Gift of Enthusiasm: When you go out shopping wear something festive for the season ~ a pin or a bright scarf or hat. Smile at everyone, spread sunshine, do your part ~ be an elf! ♥

A Gift of Wonder: Fill your child's closet with balloons so that when he or she opens it there's a big surprise!

A Gift of Love: Enroll someone in your own personal Treat-of-the-Month Club. Make a little coupon that promises one special homemade dish a month, a casserole, or a dessert ~ very good for someone who might be alone alot. ♥

The Gift of Fun: Take time to romp in the snow ~ make snow angels & snow men ~ go ice skating. Come in cold & frosty to something hot from the stove. ♥

A Gift of Contentedness:

STOP EVERYTHING & count your blessings. Have a nice glass of champagne in front of the fire with the one you love. ♥

You are the sunshine of my life! xx

The Gift of Pleasure:

Tuck a little note into lunchbox or pocket — or maybe into a suitcase. Put in a cartoon or douse it with perfume or stick on some stickers to make it look cute — say something sweet. ♥

The Gift of Yourself:

Your time can be a most precious gift — a phone call or letter — cook a lovely dinner, set a pretty table, & invite good friends. ♥

The Gift of Faith:

Before you go to bed on December 31st join hands, say a prayer & make a wish for the coming year. ♥

MIRACLES CAN HAPPEN. ♥

19

BAKED CHRISTMAS

325°

Fun for everyone ~ easy to do. ♥

Ingred: 4 c. flour, 1 c. salt, about 1½ c. water.
Mix together flour & salt. Add water ~ dough should be
stiff, not sticky. Knead 3~4 min.; if dough seems soft, knead
in more flour. Make decorations ~ in shapes of wreaths, snow
men, candy canes, Santas ~ & angels. Dig a finger in water to "glue"
pieces together. Use sharp knives, fork tines & toothpicks to help make
the decorations. Wrap thin wire around a pencil to make a hanger ~ twist
ends & stick into dough. Bake on foil-lined cookie sheets 1 hr. at 325°.
Remove; cool. Paint with watercolors. Bake again for 15 min. Paint or dip
in polyurethane or clear nail polish if you wish them to keep. ♥

Dough can be rolled
into round shapes
or oblongs; it can
be flattened or

twisted ~ & even
the tiniest pieces
keep their shapes
when baked. ♥

ANGEL BABIES

DECORATIONS

GIVE COOKIES...

... In apple baskets, lined with paper doilies or with a clean, new dishtowel.

SUGAR COOKIES

... In heart-shaped fabric-covered boxes,

or

... In old pottery bowls, wrapped in lace napkins & tied with ribbons.

... In small ice buckets,

CANDY CANE COOKIES

... In sewing baskets, tin buckets, or spread on a pretty tray...

And they taste Just As Good in a brown paper bag tied with a Christmas ribbon!

Hand write the recipe on a card & tie it with ribbon or yarn to your cookie gift ♥.

COOKIES

Mary's Mother's
SNOWBALLS

350° Makes 2½ dozen

A cookie with a surprise — it's wrapped around a Chocolate
Kiss! Mary's mother is famous for her kisses ♥.

> 2 sticks butter, softened
> 3/4 c. sugar
> 2 c. sifted flour
> 1 c. finely chopped walnuts
> 8 oz. Chocolate Kisses
> powdered sugar, for dusting

Cream butter & sugar well, until smooth. Add flour,
then walnuts. Gather dough into disk-shape & wrap in plastic.
Refrigerate at least ½ hr. Preheat oven to 350°. Remove foil
from Kisses & insert one inside a ball of dough 1" in
diameter. Make sure each Kiss is completely covered by
dough. Bake on ungreased baking sheet for about
12 min., until just cooked through. Sift over
powdered sugar while still warm. ♥

"The ancient white house with its
    steep roof and low eaves looks like
    a ship anchored in a still, white sea."
        ♥ Gladys Taber

24

CHRISTMAS WREATHS
Makes about 24

These are adorable — easy to make and look great on the cookie plate. ♥ The recipe is a version of the widely acclaimed Rice Krispie Treat. ♥

36 lg. marshmallows
1/2 c. butter
1/2 tsp. vanilla
1/4 tsp. green food coloring
3 1/2 c. cornflakes
1 pkg. candy redhots

Over medium heat, melt marshmallows & butter together. Stir in vanilla & food coloring. Fold in cornflakes & mix well. Drop by tablespoonfuls onto waxed paper. Working quickly with buttered fingers, form into little wreaths. Decorate with candies. They will firm up as they cool. ♥

"Best of all are the decorations the grandchildren have made — fat little stars and rather crooked Santas, shaped out of dough and baked in the oven."
Gladys Taber

Annie Hall's BUTTER COOKIES

350° Makes 6~8 dozen

When my friend Annie comes to dinner, her whole name is on her placecard — I just can't seem to resist! And she gave me this recipe for "the best butter cookie in the world today". (Well, we think so ♥.) You can do ANYTHING with it — twist into candy canes, roll out for cookie cutters, or drop into shapes — anything & everything & they taste fabulous ♥.

2 c. butter, softened
1½ c. sugar
4 egg yolks
2 tsp. vanilla
4½ c. unbleached flour
½ tsp. salt

Preheat oven to 350°. With an electric mixer (even the hand-held kind), cream together butter & sugar. Add egg yolks & vanilla & mix well. Sift flour & salt together & beat into butter mixture until well mixed. When ready to bake use an <u>ungreased</u> cookie sheet & place cookies 1" apart. Bake for about 10 minutes, but do not brown them. Remove cookies from cookie sheet while still warm & cool on sheets of waxed paper. Decorate, if you like ♥.

NEXT PAGE FOR COOKIE SHAPES:

Here's what you can do with *Annie Hall's* BUTTER COOKIE batter:

CANDY CANES:
Divide 3c. of dough in half. Add 1½ tsp. red food coloring to one half. Using about a tablespoon of dough, roll a 4" strip of each color (no fatter than a pencil). Place the two colored rolls side-by-side & press lightly together. Gently twist like a rope & place on ungreased cookie sheet 1" apart. Curve the top like a candy cane & bake about 10 min.; do not brown. You can sprinkle with crushed peppermint candy, if you like.

Roll Cookies:
Shape dough into rolls the width of a cookie ▭. Wrap in waxed paper & chill. Before baking, roll in chocolate shots. Slice ½" thick & bake on ungreased cookie sheet at 350° for 10 min.; do not brown.

Stars, Hearts, Circles & Jelly-filled:
Fill a pastry bag with unchilled dough & put through a "star tip" (sizes 2 & 7-9). Squeeze onto cookie sheet into the shapes you like ○ ♡ ▷ ❀ ~ just a "bloop" to make "stars" ∼ ~ fill baked centers with red jelly. Decorate these cookies with cinnamon hearts, mini chocolate morsels, colored sugar, those little silver balls, or frosting from a tube (Dec a Cake®). Bake them, same as others. Do not brown.

Cookie Cutter Cookies:
Chill dough. Roll out onto lightly floured board to thickness of ½". Cut with cookie cutters & bake as often mentioned above. Decorate in your own inimitable way ♥.

Plain Old Drop Cookies:
Just drop unchilled dough by teaspoonfuls onto ungreased cookie sheet. Bake. 350°. 10 min. Don't brown. Remove from pans immediately. Eat.

GRANDMA'S FROSTED MOLASSES COOKIES

350° Makes about 4½ doz.

A big, soft, old-fashioned cookie with a powdered sugar frosting. ♥

1 c. sugar
1 c. butter, softened
1 c. molasses
1 c. sour cream
3 tsp. baking soda

3 Tbsp. white vinegar
2 tsp. ginger
½ tsp. salt
3 eggs, beaten
4 c. unbleached flour, sifted

♥ ♥ ♥ ♥

Preheat oven to 350°. Cream butter & sugar well. Add molasses
& sour cream ~ mix well. Mix the soda with the vinegar & add it
along with ginger & salt. Stir in beaten eggs, then sifted flour.
Drop by rounded tablespoonfuls onto greased cookie sheet 2" apart.
Bake 10-12 min. Remove from pan & cool on sheets of waxed paper.
Finished cookie should be about 3½" across. Frost. ♥

Frosting

2 c. packed powdered sugar, sifted
5½ Tbsp. milk ⎫ heat
2 tsp. butter ⎭ together

1 tsp. lemon extract
2~3 Tbsp. extra hot milk

♥ ♥ ♥ ♥

With a wooden spoon beat sugar with hot milk & butter mixture.
(Put extra milk on to heat.) Beat in extract. If necessary, add additional
hot milk until creamy & spreadable. Work quickly & frost
immediately. If frosting begins to harden, beat in another drop of hot
milk. Frost thinly & let cookies dry before stacking. ♥

"Star Light, Star Bright ~ First Star I see Tonight ~
Wish I May, Wish I Might ~ Have this Wish I Wish Tonight."

CHRISTMAS NUT COOKIES

300° Makes 9 dozen

My grandma says that I should say that these aren't JUST for "Christmas Nuts" — other people like them too! This delicious cookie travels well ~ she sends them to all the *luckiest* people. 💙

1½ c. unsalted butter, softened
¼ c. Crisco, room temp.
¾ c. sugar
1 c. finely chopped nuts (walnuts, almonds, or pecans)
2 Tbsp. vanilla
4 c. unbleached, unsifted flour
powdered sugar, to roll in (not *you* ~ the cookies!) (OH WELL, IT'S CHRISTMAS — GO AHEAD. ♥)

Cream butter, Crisco & sugar together. Add other ingredients (except powdered sugar). Be sure to work in all the flour, use your hands. Roll into a large ball, wrap in plastic wrap & refrigerate several hours or overnight. Before baking, allow the dough to sit at room temp. till just soft enough to handle ~ about ½ hr. Preheat oven to 300°. Roll into small walnut-sized balls; place on ungreased cookie sheet 1" apart. Turn oven down to 275°; bake for 30~35 min. ~ they should be VERY light colored. Cool 15 min., then roll in powdered sugar. My grandma says to roll them again in powdered sugar before packing in boxes to mail. 💙

"To all, to each, a fair good night,
And pleasing dreams; and
slumbers light." 💙 Sir Walter Scott

SNOWFLAKES

Makes about 24

So pretty—powdered-sugar-shaped cookies. You'll need to have a rosette maker, available at hardware or cooking equipment stores—not expensive & worth it so your party table can have real snowflakes on it. Kids love them; me too!

1 c. cornstarch	rind of 2 lemons, grated
1/4 c. flour	2 eggs
4 tsp. sugar	1/2 c. milk
2 tsp. freshly grated nutmeg	1 qt. vegetable oil
1 tsp. ground mace	powdered sugar

Mix together cornstarch, flour, sugar, nutmeg & mace. In another bowl, beat together grated lemon rind, eggs, & milk. Pour egg mixture into dry ingredients & mix till smooth. Heat vegetable oil to 375° on a deep-frying thermometer, maintain heat over med. high flame. For each cookie, preheat iron in oil, gently place iron into batter <u>nearly</u> to top – but <u>not</u> over the top. (If batter doesn't adhere, oil is either too hot or too cold.) Lower iron slowly into oil & cook about 7 seconds, till lightly golden. Remove from oil, gently loosen with fork tines & ease off onto paper towels. Sift over powdered sugar & serve immediately. If you want to use them later: make the snowflakes, do <u>not</u> sugar, allow to cool completely & store in airtight container. Just before serving, lay cookies on cookie sheet & reheat in preheated 350° oven for 2 min. Sift sugar over—put them on serving plate & eat ♥. It's sad, but once these cookies are sugared, they <u>don't</u> keep well; however, I think they're worth the trouble & are especially nice for a buffet. ♥

Chocolate Dipped Coconut Macaroons

325° Makes about 30

Elegant-looking chewy coconut confections
edged in semi-sweet chocolate. Easy to make. ♥

2⅔ c. flake coconut, firmly packed
⅔ c. sugar
¼ c. unbleached flour
4 egg whites, unbeaten
1 c. sliced almonds
1 tsp. vanilla extract
1 tsp. almond extract

8 oz. semi-sweet chocolate, coarsely chopped

Preheat oven to 325°. Combine coconut, sugar & flour. Stir in egg whites,
almonds, vanilla & almond extract. Form balls from rounded tablespoonfuls
& place 2" apart on lightly greased cookie sheets. Bake 20-25 min. until
golden. Remove from pans while hot & allow to cool. ♥ Chocolate Edge:
Melt chocolate in double boiler, stirring until ⅔ melted; remove from
heat & continue stirring until completely melted. Dip one edge
of each cookie into chocolate & set on wax paper to allow
chocolate to set. ♥

"Chill December brings the sleet,
Blazing fire and Christmas treat."
Mother Goose ♥

FLORENTINE COOKIES

350° Makes about 40

<u>WAY</u> better than store-bought. Make your own Candied Orange Peel (good in so many Christmas recipes, see pg. 33) & you won't believe the difference ♥.

½ c. sugar
½ c. heavy cream
1¼ c. sliced almonds
¼ c. candied orange peel,
   finely chopped & homemade (p.33)
¼ c. candied citron, finely chopped

1 Tbsp. unsalted butter
3 Tbsp. flour
½ tsp. almond extract

5 oz. semi-sweet chocolate

Preheat oven to 350°. Line a cookie sheet with foil & butter it well. (If you have parchment paper, use it ~ no need to butter.) In a heavy saucepan bring the sugar & cream to boiling point ~ reduce heat & simmer 3 min., stirring. Add all other ingredients <u>except</u> chocolate &, stirring constantly, cook over low heat for 3 more minutes. Spoon mixture by rounded teaspoons onto cookie sheets ~ 2½" apart ~ they spread. Bake 8~10 min. until golden. Using a round cookie cutter (they are <u>very</u> hot) reshape cookies into circles by gently pressing in edges. Slide foil off pan & cool completely. Melt chocolate in double boiler & cool slightly. Spread a thin layer of chocolate on the smooth side of each cookie (the bottom). Immediately draw fork tines through the chocolate in an "S" pattern. Set cookies, chocolate side up, in a cool place till chocolate sets. Can be stored in an airtight container with waxed paper between layers for up to 2 weeks. ♥

COOKIES

Candied
ORANGE PEEL

Makes 1 cup

This works with all citrus & you can double this recipe so you'll have extra around to add to all sorts of Christmas recipes. It's delicious in stuffings, cookies, muffins, vegetables—any-where you want the delicious surprise of bittersweet orange.

1 c. peel (about 1½ oranges)
¼ c. water
½ c. sugar

Score oranges in quarters & remove peel. Scrape a sharp knife over skin to release oils. Cut into small squares; put in small heavy sauce-pan with enough cold water to cover. Bring to a boil, reduce heat & simmer 10 min. Drain, rinse & repeat this boiling, simmering & rinsing process 2 more times ~ this takes most of the bitterness from the peel. Add ¼ c. water plus the sugar to the peel; slowly bring to boil, stirring until sugar dissolves—reduce to simmer, watching closely until syrup is almost absorbed, stir gently until completely absorbed. Pour out onto oiled (vegetable) surface to cool & dry somewhat. Store in an airtight container in freezer or refrigerator. ♥

...AND IN THE WINTER, WILD & COLD, 'TIS MERRY, MERRY TOO.

SOMETHING SPECIAL

" "The first thing you must do," said the fairy, "is to go back into the sitting-room and find my magic wand. I'm useless without it." "
H.E. Todd

Throughout the years I have always tried to look for extra-special ways to celebrate with my friends & family — these are a few of my favorites:

For someone who is far away at Christmas time: gather friends and/or family — everybody dress up! Hold up a big sign that says "We love you, Bud" — take a picture & mail it to Bud. ♥

Send a violinist, or other instrument-toting musician, to a friend's party for a surprise serenade. ♥

Turn a child's drawing into Christmas memories; have it inexpensively printed into cards or notepads. The "right" people will consider them high art. ♥

Hold hands during grace. ♥

Ask your Grandma to describe Christmas as it was when she was a child — ask her to tell you about her parents. Tape her memories & save them for your own children. ♥

Bring Christmas cards containing news from afar to the dinner table & read them aloud. ♥

For newlyweds at Christmas — a box of really wonderful ornaments including one with the year of their 1st Christmas as husband & wife. Add to the collection yearly with a dated ornament. ♥

If you can talk someone into it: an at-home Christmas Eve wedding couldn't be more romantic, with the sparkling tree, candlelight, flowers, champagne & men in tuxedos — oooo la la! ♥

THE MAGIC OF SNOW

On December 23rd I had to go downtown to do a bit more shopping. We hadn't had any snow yet, but we were in the perfect place for Christmas — our Main Street is only 3 blocks long & the charming New England stores were decorated with tiny white lights, Christmas wreaths & Santa faces. I came out of the store with my packages just as it started to snow. It came down so soft & light; so quietly, landing on my shoulders, in my hair, on my nose. I was humming Christmas carols — everyone had smiles on their faces & Christmas had really begun.

When the snow comes, everything changes — you see special things. A horse-drawn wagon filled with happy people jingle-jangles down my street. My holly trees are heavy with snow, but the spiky green leaves & red berries still show through. There are hillsides of brightly dressed children playing with their sleds — skaters are on the ponds, their colorful scarves streaming out behind them. When I go for a walk my boots make a wonderful crunch, the chill air burns my face & I come back, refreshed, to a crackling fire & a cozy house. Time to cook something.

At night the sky is black & the stars glitter & you can smell the smoke from someone's chimney. There are flocks of wild geese, black & brown against the snow; they take off in honking unison — you can hear their wings beating the air. I love the fat bundles of winter children, their rosy red cheeks peeking out of their funny knitted caps. There's a gnarled old tree in Edgartown where they've hung loads of wax pears & on a lower branch is a brightly painted partridge.

My point is, if you don't live in snow country, try to take a Christmas vacation — get yourself a cozy house nestled in the snow — do winter things. Forget about presents — this will be the best gift of all ♥.

"THERE'S NO BUSINESS LIKE SNOW BUSINESS, LIKE NO BUSINESS I KNOW~"

Sandra Boynton

SNOW ANGELS

PLOP DOWN IN THE SNOW ON YOUR BACK ~ WAVE YOUR ARMS AND LEGS ~ GET UP AND THERE WILL BE AN ANGEL IMPRINT IN THE SNOW. ⋆ DO THE WHOLE YARD! ♥

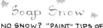

Soap Snow

NO SNOW? "PAINT" TIPS OF TREE BRANCHES WITH THIS. IT WILL HARDEN.
2 C. IVORY SNOW & ½ C. WATER ~ BEAT W/ ELECTRIC MIXER ♥.

MERRY CHRISTMAS

TAKE A PICTURE OF YOUR HOUSE IN THE SNOW, OR WRITE A MESSAGE IN THE SNOW WITH CRANBERRIES OR HOLLY BERRIES ~ TAKE A PICTURE OF IT ~ MAKE LOTS OF COPIES AND SEND THEM OUT AS CHRISTMAS POSTCARDS ♥.

MAKE SNOW PEOPLE: USE OLD HATS, SCARVES, GLOVES; PUT A FAT CANDLE IN HANDS. MAKE SCULPTURES: SWANS & DUCKS; YOU CAN USE FOOD COLORING FOR THEIR BILLS. ⋆ SNOW CASTLES: USE BUCKETS, FUNNELS, & BOXES FOR MOLDS; TWIGS & ICICLES TO DECORATE. ♥

SNOW SWEETS

SNOW CONES: POUR FRUIT JUICES OVER FRESH-FALLEN SNOW: ORANGE, CRANBERRY, OR PINEAPPLE JUICE. SUGAR ON SNOW: HEAT REAL MAPLE SYRUP TO 250°; DON'T STIR. POUR OVER A BOWL OF CLEAN SNOW. ♥

"The cold wind burns my face, and blows
It's frosty pepper up my nose."
Robt. Louis Stevenson

I'M DREAMING OF A . . .

Have a Christmas Caroling Party — have everyone arrive early so you can sing a few rounds to practice. Ask your carolers to dress in their most colorful Christmas clothes, or you can set a theme by suggesting they wear Victorian, or something from *A Christmas Carol* — more ideas:

The words! You'll be surprised at how many words you have forgotten — so hand out typed sheets with the words to favorite carols.

Invite all ages — fun for older & younger & middle ones, too. Tie a wreath of aluminum stars around children's heads.

Have lots of extra mittens, hats & scarves on hand — & a Santa hat!

Carry a flashlight — put a fat candle in a jam jar, tie it to a stick to be carried ahead.

If hay wagons & horses are available — yes! Bring blankets, hot water bottles & don't forget the thermos.

Drop by a rest home — or the hospital. — Come home, all chilly & cold, to a winter picnic in front of the fire — toast marshmallows. ♥

GIVING A WONDERFUL PARTY

A party is truly a gift from you to your friends — it's a chance to show them you love them — en masse! Life can always use a little spicing up, so give a party! Appeal to the senses — just name them off to yourself & see if you have provided for each: does it LOOK good? (fresh flowers, soft lighting, lots of candles, festive decorations); does it SOUND good? (crackling fire, ticking clocks, wonderful music); will it TASTE good? (plan the food, have crunchy & smooth, sweet & tart — make it colorful); does it FEEL good? (turn the heat a little lower than usual, give lots of hugs ♥); does it SMELL good? (things cooking, perfume & flowers — a gardenia pinned to your shoulder); & then the MAGICAL 6th sense — IMAGINATION: maybe some games, a violinist or piano player, ribbons tied to the wine glasses, luminarias or a lit pump-kin cut all over with stars on the front porch for welcome.

There are a million good reasons to have a party — you can have a theme; it can be a big blow-out New Year's party, a cozy football & soup party, a lunch, brunch, dinner or tea — keep a camera nearby & HAVE A WONDERFUL TIME!

" Christmas
won't be Christmas
without any
presents."
♥ Louisa May Alcott

HOSTESS GIFTS

Something personal or something for the house 🏠 — extravagant, simple, or funny & always with love ♥ See next page for Ideas for Collections.

MAKE A PIN FROM AN ANTIQUE STERLING SALT SPOON FOR YOUR COOK FRIENDS.

ORANGES & LEMONS

STUDDED WITH CLOVES

NO NEED TO GO EMPTY HANDED ♥

CUT OUT PAPER DOLLS FOR THE TREE

TWININGS EARL GREY TEA

TEA THINGS

A KISSING BALL

CHRISTMAS TREAT

A LEGENDARY COOKBOOK

JULIA CHILD

A FESTIVE TIE

Two trips to the moon...

A CHRISTMAS BOUQUET

TUTTO PAVAROTTI Songs & Arias DECCA 425681-2

musically speaking...

The Bishop's Wife

& in video heaven. ♥

STRIPED SOCKS

❦ IDEAS FOR COLLECTIONS ❦

· BUNNIES & EGGS · WOODEN SPOONS · CHILDREN'S DISHES
USE FOR BREAKFAST

· CHILDREN'S CHAIRS · OLD BOXES · FEATHERED
FRIENDS

· SPOTTED DOGS · CANDLE HOLDERS · TEACUPS ·

START A COLLECTION OF YOUR OWN, THEN EVERY-
ONE WILL KNOW WHAT YOU WANT FOR CHRISTMAS ♥.

CHRISTMAS SHOPPING

"The best gifts are tied with heartstrings."

WHAT HAPPENS TO PEOPLE WHO WAIT TILL THE LAST MINUTE TO SHOP?

1. They spend the entire Christmas season at, what feels like, work. Hurrying (as opposed to "bustling"); no time to stop and smell the poinsettias ♥

2. They buy the first thing they see, or "the last resort" which often turns out to be something yukky & boring, taking the fun of giving out of the season.. (Plain pitiful!)

3. To top it off, they often spend too much money (being in such a hurry) and are still paying for Christmas in April!

NO WONDER THERE ARE HUMBUGS!

Shop all year long. As you thumb through catalogs or walk through the mall, keep friends & family in mind. By Christmas you'll have a closet full of wonderful, thoughtful gifts. Instead of fighting crowds, feeling STRESS, you'll have time for visiting, playing with your children, tea time, celebrations & the spirit of Christmas. Even breakfast in bed. SLEEP. SMILING. ♥

Christmas Day

Christmas Day can go slow. I remember my uncles, one on each couch, asleep on Christmas Day. Now it's me! Here are some ideas for Christmas day ~ for fun, for relaxation, & for the memories.

➤ Give overnight guests a little breakfast in bed ~ some coffee & warm pumpkin bread with some red grapes is plenty. Put all on a tray with flowers, lace napkins ~ pamper them a little bit. ♥

➤ Give a fun Christmas gift that gets people <u>outside</u> during the day. Or, go for a walk & admire nature.

➤ Encourage people to "stop by" ~ it gives a nice break of new faces ~ stop by someone <u>else's</u> house ~ give <u>them</u> a break!

➤ Rent a movie (& a VCR) so there is something to veg-out on ~ while THEY'RE doing THAT ~ YOU can take a NAP ☺.

➤ If you invite someone to dinner, & if they want to bring something, say YES & suggest they bring whatever was traditional for them, at home. ♥

➤ Drag out dinner, eat slowly ~ linger at the table; pull out a book of carols at the end ~ sing them all ~ you'll be beautiful! Do "The Twelve Days of Christmas" ~ everybody take a part (or two). ♪

➤ Light candles, say a prayer holding hands, play music, dress up & take pictures, kiss everyone within 5 feet of the mistletoe, & keep your senses <i>alive</i> so you can remember THIS Christmas all year long. ♥

LITTLE-KNOWN CHRISTMAS SUPERSTITIONS THAT REALLY WORK

WHAT CAN I SAY?

IF A GIRL SCOUT COMES TO YOUR DOOR ANYTIME IN DECEMBER, BUY WHAT SHE HAS GOT. SHE IS AN ANGEL IN DISGUISE. ♥

DEC. 15TH, KISS A POMEGRANATE, ALL XMAS WISHES COME TRUE. ♥

DROP A SHELLED NUT IN ONE OF A TRAY OF CHRISTMAS CIDER MUGS — WHOEVER CHOOSES IT WILL PLAY A BIG ROLE IN YOUR LIFE.

DRAW A HEART IN PENCIL ON A PLAIN PIECE OF PAPER, SEND IT TO THE ONE YOU LOVE ON DEC. 21ST HE WILL BE YOURS.

HARD BOIL AN EGG CHRIST-MAS MORNING, IF IT CRACKS YOU WIN YOUR HEART'S DESIRE. (TIP: DROP ICE COLD EGG IN BOILING WATER.)

LISTEN TO "I'LL BE HOME ♪ FOR CHRISTMAS" 3 TIMES IN A ROW, AND YOU WILL BE. (IF NOT, TRY CLICKING YOUR HEELS TOGETHER 3 TIMES.)

DROP 3 CRANBERRIES ON THE GROUND ~ THE FURTHEST ONE OUT DIRECTS YOU TO THE ONE YOU LOVE. (DROP WITH A CERTAIN FLAMBOYANCE.) ●

DURING THE CHRISTMAS SEASON OF YOUR 16TH YEAR IF A BABY SMILES AT YOU ~ TRUE LOVE IS NEAR BY ♥

CHRISTMAS
LOVE

IF YOU FIND AN ORANGE IN THE TOE OF YOUR CHRISTMAS STOCKING, VALENTINE'S DAY WILL BE GLORIOUS ♥ (AS OPPOSED TO CHRISTMAS :-))

PULL OUT A GRAY HAIR ON CHRISTMAS DAY AND A CHILD WILL KISS YOU. POSSIBLY ALL DAY LONG. ♥ ♥ ♥

ON CHRISTMAS EVE PUT THREE PINK PEPPERCORNS UNDER YOUR LOVER'S PILLOW; HE WILL DO THE CHRISTMAS DISHES. ♥

THE BIG BOOK OF WELL-KNOWN FACTS

SMELL A YELLOW ROSE THE MORNING OF THE 17TH OF DEC. & THERE'S A GOOD CHANCE YOU'LL GET DIAMONDS FOR XMAS. (WELL-KNOWN FACT.) ♥

"A little nonsense now and then
Is relished by the wisest men."
♥ Anonymous

46

The love in your heart
wasn't put there to stay,
love isn't love
till it's
given
away.

"Ah friends, dear friends, as
    years go on & heads get gray,
how fast the guests do go!
Touch hands, touch hands,
    with those that stay.
    Strong hands to weak,
        old hands to young,
Around the Christmas board
        touch hands."

Wm. H. H. Murray

KISS ME!

Send your name & address to me (Susan Branch) at P. O. Box 2463B, Vineyard Haven, MA 02568 & I'll put you on my mailing list! ♥

HO HO HO

U.S. MAIL

KISS